A WAY OF LIFE:

AN APPRENTICESHIP WITH FRANK LLOYD WRIGHT

by LOIS DAVIDSON GOTTLIEB

A WAY OF LIFE:

AN APPRENTICESHIP WITH FRANK LLOYD WRIGHT

by LOIS DAVIDSON GOTTLIEB

First published in Australia in 2001 by
The Images Publishing Group Pty Ltd
ACN 059 734 431
6 Bastow Place, Mulgrave, Victoria, 3170
Telephone (61 3) 9561 5544 Facsimile (61 3) 9561 4860
Email: books@images.com.au

National Library of Australia
Cataloguing-in-Publication data

        Gottlieb, Lois Davidson.
        A way of life: an apprenticeship with Frank Lloyd Wright.

        ISBN 1 86470 096 3.

        1. Wright, Frank Lloyd, 1867–1959. 2. Gottlieb, Lois Davidson, 1926– — Influence. 3. Gottlieb, Lois Davidson,
        1926– — Career in architecture. 4. Architects — United States. 5. Architecture, Modern — 20th century —
        United States. I. Title.

        720.973

Edited by Renée Otmar, Otmar Miller Consultancy Pty Ltd, Melbourne
Designed by The Graphic Image Studio Pty Ltd, Mulgrave, Australia
Film by Pageset Pty Ltd, Melbourne
Printed by Paramount Printing Co. Ltd, Hong Kong.

Contents

Acknowledgments

This book goes back to the first step in my career as an architect. There were many people who helped make it happen.

The first one, whose name I have long since forgotten, was a professor at Stanford University who took me to see the Hanna House. The house was designed by Frank Lloyd Wright, and I was so thrilled that my teacher urged me to ask Mr. Wright to join his fellowship.

The second was, of course, Mr. Wright himself, to whom this book is dedicated. He changed my life forever with the way of life to which he exposed me for the year-and-a-half I lived at Taliesin and Taliesin West with him, his family, and the other apprentices.

Then came my marriage to Robert S. Gottlieb, and my two children, Karen and Mark. All three have been endlessly supportive of my various projects, including an exhibition of the photographs and the book resulting from it.

More recently, but for a long time, two other friends have urged me to publish my photographs and thoughts about my various adventures. One was Marilyn Shaw, a guest lecturer in a class I gave at the University of California in Riverside, California. The other, Eva Soltes—a film maker who produced and edited a film for my husband—was excited about these photos and produced a video of the photographs I took during construction of a house I had designed. This film was bought by the American Institute of Architects (AIA) in Washington, DC for its library. Through this contact in the library I was introduced to Linnea Hamer of the Octagon Museum at the AIA. She became interested in my Taliesin slides, and produced a beautiful exhibition of these photographs.

It was at the AIA in Washington, DC that Paul Latham of The Images Publishing Group in Melbourne, Australia saw the photographs and proposed the idea of publishing them in a book.

The quality of the photographs is due to Eastman Kodak film, which has retained its color and definition for over 50 years, the Lightwaves company in San Francisco, which digitally printed my slides, and the work of The Graphic Image Studio in Melbourne.

Although I am the one who took the photos, this book would not have happened without the support and help in various ways of all these people.

My many thanks,
Lois Davidson Gottlieb

Kitchen entry, Taliesin West

Preface

by Bruce Brooks Pfeiffer
Director, Frank Lloyd Wright Archives
and Vice President, Frank Lloyd Wright Foundation

In 1902, Frank Lloyd Wright designed a new building for the Hillside Home School, near the town of Spring Green, Wisconsin. The school had been founded in 1886 by Wright's maternal aunts, Ellen and Jane Lloyd Jones. The school's program was progressive and radical for its time. Boys and girls, aged five to eighteen, lived in a "home" environment, with education and daily chores equally balanced—but with a strong emphasis on respect for and closeness to nature, in all its varying aspects. The agrarian life was also built into the school's curriculum. Headed by the founders' brother, James Lloyd Jones, the children were taught to care for the farm animals and to be responsible for a plot in the kitchen gardens.

In 1915, the Hillside Home School was forced to close due to financial reasons. The founders then transferred ownership of the property and its buildings to their nephew, Frank Lloyd Wright. They extracted the promise from him that he would someday make use of the buildings in an educational endeavor. He was unable to honor that promise until many years later.

In 1928 Frank Lloyd Wright began with a proposal for the Hillside Home School for the Allied Arts, in association with the University of Wisconsin. The program was to embrace all the arts. This proposal proved so ambitious, however, that it had to be abandoned. Eventually, Wright succeeded in 1932 in founding a new school for architectural study, the Taliesin Fellowship. The architect's wife, Olgivanna, believed he should not only build buildings, but should also teach future builders, and so, the school program was designed to "build the builders of monuments."

Preface continued

Midway barn, Taliesin

Twenty-three young men and women arrived in mid-October of 1932 to take up life as apprentices to Frank Lloyd Wright. Their tuition dollars helped to provide the means for them to begin renovating the now dilapidated Hillside Home School buildings. In spite of the Depression and the fact that Wright had little or no architectural work coming in, the school survived. In 1941, with the Fellowship entering its eighth year, Wright explained the philosophy behind it in a Taliesin publication entitled **Our Work**:

"The Fellowship must and does stand together in atmosphere free from pretence. It stands upon 'soil' which will nourish sincerity of character and purpose. Each Fellow may honestly possess that, at least, as a basis for cultivation of talent… All are here together with me in a spontaneous way of life in surroundings pointing in the direction of that interpretation … Apprenticeship back there in the feudal middle-ages was something like this one at Taliesin but with an important difference: the apprentice then was his master's servant: at democratic Taliesin he is his master's comrade. The apprentice is actively engaged with his master, together with a closely limited group of others like-minded, in the spirit of timely creation."(**Taliesin**, February, 1941)

Fellowship life was a life of shared communal activities, inspired by one of the greatest artists of the 20th century. The apprentices shared the work in the kitchen and in the gardens, on construction and on maintenance projects at the two Taliesins. They shared picnics and field trips, music and dance performances. But they also worked hard in the studio on actual commissions, including the most famous—Fallingwater, the Johnson Wax Administration Building, and the Guggenheim Museum.

The Taliesin Fellowship grew to sixty-five apprentices, and flourished until Wright's death in 1959. Olgivanna, not wanting to relinquish her husband's concept of hands-on learning in the training of architects, was determined that the Taliesin Fellowship would continue.

With the dedicated support of a nucleus of several apprentices who elected to remain at Taliesin, the school continued under her guidance until her death in 1985. Renamed The Frank Lloyd Wright School of Architecture, the school continues today to educate new generations of international architects.

Lois Davidson Gottlieb entered the Taliesin Fellowship as an apprentice to Frank Lloyd Wright in 1948, remaining at Taliesin for a year and a half. Along with the other apprentices she took part in all aspects of Fellowship life. At the same time she actively participated in the architectural work going on in the drafting room with Frank Lloyd Wright.

Fortunately, for posterity, she had brought along her camera. Of course, many other apprentices had their cameras as well, but limited their photography mostly to Wright and his buildings. Lois, on the other hand, made a fine record, not only of the two Taliesins, but also of the activities of the life going on around her.

This book, then, adds enormously to the study of Frank Lloyd Wright the architect, and also documents what he set out to accomplish in this endeavor of **building the builders of monuments**.

Bruce Brooks Pfeiffer
Taliesin West

Wing of Taliesin

Living a Dream: Lois Davidson Gottlieb, Architect

Lois Davidson Gottlieb exemplifies the tradition of the Taliesin Fellowship at its best.

Lois Davidson was born in San Francisco, California on November 13, 1926. As an undergraduate in Stanford University's pre-architecture program, where she would earn her Bachelor of Arts, Davidson saw Frank Lloyd Wright's Hanna House (1936) on the university campus. For Davidson, this first encounter with a building designed by the famous American architect strengthened her desire to be an architect, and gave her the resolve to build something as beautiful. As she would later recall, "It was as if I'd never heard a note of music before and suddenly heard a symphony."[1]

Driven by a desire to learn everything she could about Wright's architecture, Davidson applied and was accepted as an apprentice to the Taliesin Fellowship, which had its winter headquarters near Scottsdale, Arizona (Taliesin West). Here, in 1948 she met Wright and began a two-year journey of work and study that would shape her future and her professional career. She was to discover that, as the title of this book so aptly states, architecture could be "a way of life."

No better anecdote tells of the immediate impact that the Taliesin experience had on Davidson than her introduction to the Fellowship: "When I first joined Frank Lloyd Wright's Taliesin Fellowship [in 1948], it was winter and Mr. and Mrs. Wright and their group of apprentices were living at their desert camp in Arizona. I arrived, with sleeping bag and baggage, and Mrs. Wright led me into the desert to a tiny, pyramidal tent. She said, 'This is your tent and it is up to you to make it beautiful.'"[2]

Mark Gottlieb residence

Learning how to make things beautiful is a charge that Davidson took to heart; she found that she could be equally at home weaving a cloth at the loom, preparing jam in the kitchen, harvesting corn in the fields, or contributing her design and drafting skills in the studio. At that time (1948), she worked on the Pratt house in Michigan and the Walker house in Carmel, California.

Even though she continued her professional training at the Harvard Graduate School of Design, Davidson found her return to academia terribly disappointing after her two-year apprenticeship with Wright. Above all, Davidson had learned at Taliesin that beauty in architecture is a matter of principle that every architect has to discover for himself or herself, so that in each creation "form is allowed to follow feeling."[3]

Her own work in the years that followed gave tangible expression to Davidson's interpretation of those principles. By now married to Robert S. Gottlieb, her first California houses—Val-Goeshen, Inverness (1951), Robert S. Gottlieb, San Francisco (1955), and Robert S. Gottlieb, Riverside (1964)—all share a reverence for nature, careful attention to materials and details, and celebration of the activities that define the sanctuary of the home, true to the Wrightian spirit of an "Organic Architecture." With these buildings Lois Davidson Gottlieb launched her career as a residential designer—the professional title she prefers because it represents her most significant architectural work.

Although she designed other distinguished residences in California, such as the Mackey and Beals houses in Riverside (1966 and 1967, respectively), Gottlieb's reputation as an architect grew during the following 20 years, thanks to a steady flow of commissions in the states of Washington, Idaho, and Arizona. Some of her best known designs belonging to this period include the Hansen House in Seattle, Washington (1978), the Lynn House in Ketchum, Idaho (1980), and the Harrah Energy Efficient House in Sedona, Arizona (1981). In the process, Gottlieb gained well-deserved recognition as a "pioneer," not only because she is a woman designer in a profession traditionally dominated by men, but also because she is one of the few women to have been apprenticed to Frank Lloyd Wright who succeeded in charting

Living room

an independent career for herself. And all this was done while raising two children—Karen Gottlieb and Mark Gottlieb—as well as being involved in her husband's career as an ethnomusicologist, which included the family living in India and Austria eight times for as much as a year several times.

Gottlieb's professional career, spanning more than 50 years, is fully documented in her papers, which were donated in 1997 to the International Archive of Women in Architecture at Virginia Tech, in Blacksburg, Virginia.

Gottlieb would be the first to recognize that the influence of Frank Lloyd Wright has been present in her work through the years, and remains even today a source of inspiration. At the first major retrospective exhibition of her work, titled "Lois D. Gottlieb: Continuing the Legacy of Frank Lloyd Wright" and held at Virginia Tech in 1998, for example, she acknowledged that Wright's influence continues to be reflected in her work and philosophy of design, because she believes that "architecture is a synthesis of the needs of the client with the site and materials... [and is] a reflection of the family that lives there."[4]

Yet, through a journey of personal discovery, Gottlieb was able to interpret these Wrightian principles in her own way, as described in her beautifully written theoretical book, **Environment and Design in Housing** (1965). Appropriately enough, in this work Gottlieb fully comes into her own by focusing on housing as a part of one's total environment, and shows how design and style develop out of the way in which each person, family, or civilization creates an environment to satisfy its particular needs and interests. As she eloquently puts it, the challenge is of creating one's style—"by making the dwelling as a personal expression."[5]

When in 1991 Gottlieb was asked by her son Mark and his wife Sharon to design their new house in Fairfax Station, Virginia, she welcomed the opportunity and embarked on what turned out to be the most ambitious project of her professional career to date: a 10,000 square foot, two-level residence wrapped around a hill which overlooked a beautiful lake. At once Gottlieb reviewed the three components that she had learned to identify as being of utmost importance when designing a residence—the needs of the owner, advantages and limitations of the site, and the materials available. When the house was completed five years later, it was evident that the architect had achieved a masterpiece that reflected the principles that had guided her entire professional career. Gottlieb poured all of her creative talent into this project, revealing an inquisitive eye and a predilection for using inventive materials and methods of construction. Of paramount importance was the role played by the architect, not only as designer but also as director of every phase of construction at the site. The fact that the client was an inventor of high-technology consumer products inspired Gottlieb to experiment with contemporary innovations in building assembly and materials, coupled with the implementation of a "smart house" computer system for security that would be integrated with traditional finish materials of brick and wood. The construction, of standardized, factory made materials, provided low maintenance and energy efficiency. New materials such as "Trex" decking (made of sawdust and melted plastic bags) were used for balcony flooring, and materials such as "ICE" (blocks made of recycled plastic bottles) provided the form work for concrete walls. The structural components included glue-laminated wood beams and engineered wood products whose manufacture produced relatively no waste.

Spatial continuity was achieved through an integration of bedrooms and other living spaces in a single volume wrapped around the hill of a five-acre southern slope. Natural light, Wright's "beautifier of space," was allowed to enter through generous windows and a 250-foot skylight, so that in the interior no one is ever more than 6 feet away from sunlight. Special homage was also paid to Gottlieb's **lieber meister** and mentor through the elegant incorporation of Wright's Francis W. Little House[6] art glass doors (purchased from an antique dealer) in the main entrance of the house. In addition, meticulous landscaping enriched with water fountains inside and outside complements the natural setting—true to the conception of the house as a totally integrated work of art.

Gottlieb wrote: "When creating a house for someone, I try to make it a portrait of the client executed in my own style. In this case, the client happens to be my son and daughter-in-law, who have four children ...

Entry

"My challenge was to create a dwelling that combines 21st century technology with traditional charm ... My apprenticeship with Frank Lloyd Wright taught me to be harmonious with nature and to take full advantage of a beautiful setting."[7]

Luckily, in this instance the entire process of design and construction of the Mark and Sharon Gottlieb House was documented in an extraordinary video titled **Building a Dream: A Family Affair**, produced and narrated by the architect herself.[8] In it, Mark Gottlieb comments, "I always knew one day we'd have a perfect house and that my mom would design it." It was a project, no doubt, where an "ideal architect" worked for "ideal clients."

It would seem that throughout her career Lois Gottlieb met other ideal clients for whom she designed beautiful houses. Now 74, and still practising, may she meet many more ideal clients!

Humberto Rodríguez-Camilloni, PhD
Professor of Architecture and Director
Henry H. Wiss Center for Theory and History of Art and Architecture
Virginia Tech
Blacksburg, Virginia
September 26, 2000

Koi Pond

16

Notes

1 Quoted by Patricia D. Rogers, "Wright: From One Generation to the Next," **The Washington Post**, Thursday, May 11, 2000, p.7.

2 Lois D. Gottlieb, **Environment and Design in Housing**, New York: The Macmillan Company, 1965, p.V.

3 I am paraphrasing here Frank Lloyd Wright's statement "form follows feeling" in response to Louis H. Sullivan's famous dictum "form follows function."

4 Quoted from the speaker and event description for special exhibition, "Lois D. Gottlieb: Continuing the Legacy of Frank Lloyd Wright," held at Virginia Tech, Blacksburg, Virginia, March 16–April 5, 1998.

5 Gottlieb, op.cit., p.75.

6 This 1912 house, designed by Frank Lloyd Wright in Deephaven, Minnesota, was demolished in 1972. The reconstructed living room of the house is in the Metropolitan Museum of Art, New York City.

7 Lois D. Gottlieb, personal correspondence, March 1998.

8 Lois D. Gottlieb, Executive Producer, and Eva Soltes, Producer–Director, **Building a Dream: A Family Affair**, video, San Francisco: Lois Gottlieb, 1998.

Taliesin, Spring Green, Wisconsin

Introduction

In 1947 I was a student at Stanford University. I was about to graduate and did not know what I was going to do with myself. It was required that I have a major. Since a combination of engineering and art was available, called Pre-Architecture, this seemed a most likely choice. Engineering was easy for me, and I really enjoyed art.

During my last quarter at Stanford I took a class in which every week we went to look at a modern house located near the campus. Most of these were nice, but uninspiring. In the final week we went to see Frank Lloyd Wright's Hanna House. I was stunned and enchanted. It was as though I had never heard music before and here was confronted with the visual equivalent of a Beethoven symphony. I had to do something about this!

I talked to my teacher, and he encouraged me to write to Mr. Wright and ask to join the Taliesin Fellowship. When I asked what kind of school this was, my teacher replied, "It's not a school, it's a way of life." At the time I didn't know what that meant, but I was undaunted and wrote to Mr. Wright. I was accepted into the Fellowship, and I lived at Taliesin in Spring Green, Wisconsin, and Taliesin West in Scottsdale, Arizona for a year and a half.

In 1949, Mr. Wright designed a small house for his daughter, Iovanna, and guests. Today, it is still being used as a guest house. My husband and I stayed there a few years ago. Much had changed at Taliesin and Taliesin West since I had lived there.

In 1948, most of the apprentices in the Fellowship lived in tents scattered about the neighboring desert at Taliesin West. I lived in a tent for the first year I was there. The following year I had a room. We all built our own furniture and decorated our rooms and tents. Being an architect was not just a profession, it was a way to make all aspects of living more beautiful and compatible with the environment.

At Taliesin we learned by doing. Mr. Wright was always there, supervising the building projects as well as the drawings. There were no formal lectures or classes. If one of us didn't know how to do something, there was always someone around who had been there longer and could be of help. We were able to approach Mr. Wright for his advice—he always knew what to do.

I remember one incident when Mr. Wright asked me to re-do a window. I started out on the project, doing what he suggested, but soon came up with an idea of my own which I thought better. When I explained

Tea circle

my idea to Mr. Wright, I was delighted with his reaction: "That's a wonderful idea. I'm jealous that I didn't think of it myself." That was a warm-hearted response to a 20-year-old from one who by then was 80 years old, and who considered himself to be the world's greatest architect.

We also learned from each other. Many of the apprentices were fine craftsmen. Some previously had worked as professional carpenters, while others were knowledgeable in metal work or other specialized fields. Among other things, I happened to know how to weave. Others there knew how to draw wonderfully, and some even had prior experience in farming. So we shared our knowledge and expertise with each other. As far as managing the kitchen, there were numerous cookbooks, but with 50 apprentices from different backgrounds, there was always someone who knew how to get something done.

Taliesin was not like a university. It was for real. Someone was going to live in the buildings we were designing. These were serious projects so we all gave them our best efforts.

No one bothered to introduce anyone. One just turned up at some activity, saw what was going on, and offered to help. One of my first activities was helping to stretch canvas over wooden frames. Then I helped with making hassocks for the living room. I poured concrete and carried rocks to put in the concrete. Eventually someone let me do some lettering on his drawings. After this I designed cabinets for a kitchen by looking at designs used in other houses. And ultimately I did the drawings for a whole house by consulting drawings done for other houses and also consulting those apprentices who knew more than I did. All this was done under Mr. Wright's supervision.

On Sunday mornings after breakfast, Mr. Wright would talk to us as a group. These talks were generally philosophical in nature, rather than focused on architecture. I believe the timing for these informal talks derived from the fact that Mr. Wright's father had been a minister, and that he had been raised listening to Sunday morning discussions of some sort. (Mr. Wright was no longer interested in organized religion. I remember watching a television program in which Mr. Wright was being interviewed. His response to a question concerning organized religion was "Why organize it?")

My experience at Taliesin was that the apprentices all got along very well. Naturally, everyone cultivated special friendships that developed over time. Yet, I never sensed any major problems arising. I think this was because we all had common goals and were inspired and thrilled to be

there. We all got to know each other by working together and being together at meal times, weekend activities, social occasions and other events. But there was no effort in a formal sense to bring people together. At Taliesin I learned that people from different backgrounds and countries can get along well if they have a common goal and a great leader.

Many of the apprentices later became architects. Some became professors of architecture. Others are now working in related fields. Mansinh Rana, from New Delhi, India, became the head architect for the government of India. Paolo Soleri, from Italy, now runs his own fellowship program in Arizona. Walter Olids designed the wonderful Weyerhouser Company headquarters building near Tacoma, Washington, while he worked for Skidmore, Owens and Merrill. Undoubtedly, there are many others doing amazing things. These I have mentioned here happened to be the ones I knew when I was at Taliesin.

There was only one other woman apprentice when I was there who later became an architect, Jane Duncombe. She has since worked on many excellent buildings in Northern California. The other women at Taliesin were the wives of the apprentices, Mrs. Wright, her sister-in-law, and Mr. and Mrs. Wright's daughter, Iovanna. Mr. Wright wanted more women to come to Taliesin as apprentices, but in those days not many were interested in architecture or becoming part of a communal situation. In 1948 Mr. Wright's work was still considered to be strange and unacceptable by many. The fellowship was then generally looked upon as being unconventional by traditional society.

When I arrived in 1948, I think I was the only apprentice with a camera. This was a $25 Kodak Bantam, which produced 40-millimeter color slides. I was thrilled with the architecture at Taliesin and Taliesin West, and took many photographs. I was equally delighted with all the activities of my fellow apprentices, so I photographed these as well. This book is my record of the Taliesin way of life.

One may wonder why the Taliesin Fellowship has not produced another Frank Lloyd Wright. While at Taliesin I went to visit a Frank Lloyd Wright house in the Mid-west, and was as thrilled with this house as I had been with the Hanna House. When I got back to Taliesin I told Mr. Wright how thrilled I was and asked, "What is it that makes it so beautiful?"

He answered, "It's magic."

Frank Lloyd Wright had offered all the apprentices a tremendous amount in many ways, but to me he seemed to be the only architect who was able to produce that magic time after time.

Taliesin, Spring Green, Wisconsin
1948–49

A view of the Taliesin valley

The Wisconsin River, bordering Taliesin. Taliesin is located 30 miles west of Madison, Wisconsin.

Taliesin, the land which Mr. Wright inherited from his family. "Taliesin" is Welsh for "shining brow." The house is located on the brow of the hill seen in the background. The hay-cocks in the foreground were built by the apprentices, and this corn was later used to feed the cows in the winter.

Mr. Wright designed "Romeo and Juliet" for his aunts in 1896. It was one of his first projects.

The Hillside buildings and the drafting rooms used by Mr. Wright and the apprentices. The original buildings were used for the Hillside Home School, owned by Mr. Wright's aunts.

These buildings, constructed of sandstone, date from 1902.

Momentoes in the garden at Hillside: highly ornamented concrete blocks (c. 1910), and statues from the Midway Gardens, built in 1913. (This has since been demolished.)

The driveway to the main house, located on the hill at Taliesin.

The upper dam, used to produce electricity. Here the two heavy columns embrace the dam wall.

The parking area at Taliesin. Behind this was the barn for the horses. In the days before bulldozers it was probably easier to construct a wooden terrace rather than cut into the hill.

Part of Mr. Wright's collection of oriental art

The limestone quarry in the fall. The walls at Taliesin reflect nature's patterns at the quarry.

This masonry supports both floors and roofs. Areas in between are cantilevered in wood.

The exterior of the living room. The lower roof covered a stairway to a lower floor of guest rooms. In the background was a massive chimney and the low roof of an alcove used to house a piano.

The room with the cantilevered balcony was set aside for Iovanna, Mr. and Mrs. Wright's daughter.

The balcony is constructed around the tree. The masonry chimney supports the cantilevered floors and roof.

The same area, several years later

Looking down into the entry court

The entry to the main house at Taliesin. An oriental carving is incorporated into the door. Mr. Wright was a master at incorporating meaningful things and works of art into his architecture.

A view of the living room, with chairs designed by Mr. Wright. Sunday night dinner in the living room was followed by listening to chamber music.

From the living room the space flows into the hallway and onto the balcony. "Modern" architecture is often considered to be something cold and stark, but this is surely not the case at Taliesin, which reflects Mr. Wright's love of natural materials and his interest in ornamentation.

Each apprentice was assigned an area of the building to keep clean and decorate with flowers, branches etc. Saturday mornings were devoted to housekeeping.

Another building at Taliesin.

Every room here is on a different level. This gave us a feeling of privacy. The windows are designed to be integrated into the overall design—not just holes punched into a wall.

Many apprentices raised crops. I raised an acre of corn. After lunch each day, I would go out to till the soil for about an hour. Since I grew up in the middle of San Francisco, this was another new experience for me. This introduction to agriculture later led me to supply my family with a variety of foods over the years and in the various places we've lived—citrus fruit, berries, vegetables, and even oysters from Puget Sound, 2000 miles west of Taliesin.

One of the dairy herd—probably my closest encounter with a cow!

Bill Patrick, having just returned from serving in the army in Japan, hoeing squash in his Japanese clothes.

I recently attended Bill's 80th birthday party at Midglen, near San Francisco. He and three other apprentices built Midglen in about 1950. It has since been expanded to include additional living quarters and work spaces for his two sons and their families. One son is an architect and the other is a building contractor. Following in the Fellowship tradition, they all work together.

Mansinh Rana came from India. Here he is helping me pick the corn I raised.

Mansinh later returned to India, and ultimately became head architecture for the Government of India. His son is now a very fine architect in New Delhi.

Dennis Stevens harvesting field corn.

The corn was ground up for storage in the silo.

Here Nils Schweizer loads the silo.

Edward Abeywarden cutting parsley for dinner.

We apprentices all took turns at cooking. On Saturday nights we served ice cream for dessert. Those who helped to churn it were rewarded with an extra bowl.

Enjoying our Saturday afternoon extra ice cream treat.

Jane Duncomb and other apprentices performed in a recorder ensemble. Jane is now a practising architect in Northern California.

Marcelle Grandjany, one of the world's leading harpists, came to Taliesin for the summer. Mr. Wright frequently invited professional musicians to be his guests.

Mr. and Mrs. Wright

Mr. and Mrs. Wright. Mr. Wright was about 80 years old when I took this photo.

Mr. and Mrs. Wright came from the main house at Taliesin to Hillside for their meals, and also so Mr. Wright could work in the drafting room.

Wednesday evenings were set aside for picnics. This is
Eric Wright, Mr. Wright's grandson, holding a steak.
He is the son of Lloyd Wright, and is now
an architect in Southern California.

The theater, where dinner was served on Saturday evenings, with a movie afterwards.

This panel at the left is ornamented with an excerpt from Beethoven's "Pathetique" Sonata. Beethoven was Mr. Wright's favorite composer. On the right is a quartet stand. Four music stands are combined onto a single pedestal.

Intellectual activity and entertainment were also an important part of our lives at Taliesin. An addition to the Hillside Theater was attached to the main theater building on the left, and to the tree on the right.

As a student at Stanford, I had studied flashing, a waterproofing device, but really had no idea about how this worked. After spending several days on top of a ladder, chiselling a slot into a stone wall, I understood completely what flashing was all about.

Bill Patrick, Sean O'Hare, and Don Fairweather constructing the roof for the addition to the theater.

John Crider learned to operate a bulldozer while in the army. Here he levels the area for the construction of the "round-house," a building to be used for storing farm vehicles.

The foundation for the "round-house" was made of limestone. George Haas was Mr. Wright's only professional employee. He was both a mason and a butcher, and taught us masonry. Here he is at the quarry.

Lee Kawahara sets up the centerpost for the "round-house."
All measurements were taken from this center point.
In the background is the milk house.

Lee Kawahara and Peter Mathews watch Mr. Wright at work on the site, making changes to the plans for one of the farm buildings.

Peter Mathews and Sheng Pao building the "round-house" foundation. Peter and his wife came from England. Sheng Pao, from China, also came with his wife. He had worked as an engineer on the Burma Road. Sheng died years ago, but his wife still lives in West Virginia.

The structure of the "round-house" before the roof was added.

The same circular theme was used for the hay rack. For Mr. Wright the design of a hay rack was as important a consideration as the design of any other structure.

A little house for a sheepherder—a masonry foundation, wooden floor, and a cantilevered roof

Calvin Stempel, from Panama, working on the roof.

Painting the pig houses

As winter approached, the entire Fellowship would pack up and leave for Taliesin West. On the way we camped at a park in Kansas City.

This brand-new Cadillac, almost unrecognizable by now, belonged to the conductor of the Chicago Symphony, Artur Rodzinsky. He wanted the car to be shipped west, and Mr. Wright offered to have the apprentices drive it there for him. Little did Mr. Rodzinsky know we would each be traveling with all our worldly possessions!

Mr. Wright also owned a moving van, which would be used to transport larger things to Arizona, as well as all the food we had raised and canned during the summer at Taliesin.

Taliesin West, Scottsdale, Arizona
1948–49

A sign on the road near Taliesin, 18 miles from Scottsdale.

Taliesin West is set against the hills. It was built entirely by Mr. Wright's apprentices. Its initial concept, started in 1938, was a tented camp. These tents were subsequently glorified and transformed into the winter camp, as seen in these photographs. In the distance, on top of the hill, is the tent which Paffard Keating-Clay erected for himself when he first came to Taliesin West.

The first entry gate to Taliesin West. All the walls at Taliesin West were constructed by means of building forms. We placed rocks against the insides of the forms, and then poured in concrete and rubble behind them.

Also at the entry, around 1965. By now, with more power and electricity available, it was possible to use water for cooling and ornamental purposes, and for planting.

Mr. Wright's office. We used a jeep to go out into the surrounding desert to collect rocks.

The terrace and planting areas around Mr. Wright's office were contained within concrete parapet walls.

Architectural ornaments mimic the cactus forms of the desert.

The drafting room, as seen from the end. The same, but larger structure as was used for Mr. Wright's office.

The vault at the end of the drafting room was used to protect the drawings from fire and other damage.

The wall of the drafting room. The poles could be used to raise the top canvas panels to let out the hot air.

The walkway in front of the drafting room. The beams and diagonal braces form intricate shadow patterns. The doors, originally of white canvas, were later painted red to cover up accumulated dirt and handprints.

The series of redwood beams covering this walkway provided both a feeling of shade and shelter, and an aesthetic experience created by the shadow patterns.

The same walkway 15 years later; steel beams replaced the weathered redwood beams, and bougainvillea vines replaced the cactus plants.

All plants were placed in well-defined areas. Canvas panels high on the walls opened up to provide ventilation and escape for the hot air. This was a practical solution before the days of air conditioning.

The original theater on the left, and a water storage tank on the right. Cactus plants were transplanted from the desert and used in landscaping. Mr. Wright's idea was to incorporate the beauty of the desert and its plant forms into his architecture, rather than to change the desert into a vast, mid-western lawn, as was generally the custom in Arizona.

Apprentices putting the final touches on the water tower.

Looking out from the dining room one could see the desert landscape. The overhead glass panels exposed the sky and at the same time revealed the sparks emanating from the fireplace. This created a beautiful effect in the evening.

A terrace overlooking the desert

The original bell tower

The renovated bell tower; the broken bell was replaced with plough discs.

The original theater was designed to look like a Native American **kiva**, a ceremonial building usually enclosed and without windows. The fireplace was lowered several inches; it was filled with water and flowers during hot weather. A fan installed in the chimney blew cool air from the water. In cold weather, logs were burned in the fireplace.

A simple architectural concept: all the utilities are located at the center of the house, with the living areas placed around the outside.

Ted Bower and Don Fairweather screeding (smoothing out and leveling) the concrete floor.

Today, Ted still works as an architect (in Seattle), while Don designs huge hotels all over the world.

Building the chimney. In the foreground is Edward Abeywarden from Ceylon. There were about 50 apprentices, representing 27 countries.

A close-up of the chimney construction. Ted Bower and Leonard Spangenberg pack the concrete at the top.

The completed chimney. Paffard Keating-Clay's white tent can be seen in the distance on top of the hill.

The upper sections of the window areas are covered with canvas to diffuse the sunlight. The lower parts, made of glass, permit an unobstructed view of the desert.

The guest house 15 years later, and the outdoor theater. This theater was used primarily for dance, which interested Mrs. Wright in particular.

Curtis Besinger surveying the roof for the new theater (1949).
This theater was much larger than the original one.
The construction concept was simple. First, a hole was
bulldozed for the foundation, then the floor and walls were
covered with concrete. A concrete slab was used for the roof.
This slab was supported by the wall on one side and by
elaborate posts on the other side.

A temporary wooden structure was built; this form supported the pouring of the reinforced concrete roof.

Mansinh Rana applying shellac to the forms for the concrete posts, so the concrete would not stick to them.

Wes Peters and Joe Fabris lowering the forms into place. Wes and Joe spent most of their lives at Taliesin. Wes is no longer alive, but Joe still lives at Taliesin, though he is now retired.

Sand was collected at a wash (a dry riverbed) in the desert, and used to make concrete.

Steve Oyakawa sitting on the truck while unloading the sand at the cement-mixer.

The heat became more intense as summer approached.

Tony Capucelli delivering the concrete.

Fende Askell, from Turkey, screeding the concrete.

Fende and Paffard Keating-Clay pulling nails from the boards so they could be used again.

A shaded area where we had lunch. The two-layered roof provided a means for the hot air to escape.

This pool was used both for swimming and for storing water in case of fire. Mr. Wright said this was his favorite photo of Taliesin West.

The door to the living room was made of overlapping boards. The entry was small and dark; this darkness accentuated the brilliance of the living room, with its canvas roof.

The interior of the living room. One of my first projects was to make hassocks for this room.

This is my favorite glass wall. It is located at one end of the living room. The chairs came from a furniture store. One of the apprentices wove the afghan covers, and others made the hassocks as well as constructing the entire room.

The end of the living room

The front of the living room opened onto a small garden for Mr. and Mrs. Wright.

A model of the Loeb House made for the Museum of Art in New York, being prepared by Curtis Besinger and Richard Salter. Paolo Soleri carved the small wooden figures. The waterfalls were made of plastic and beads.

Mr. Wright set a chinese plaque into the wall, and combined this with his red square signature tile.

Lois Davidson weaving at the loom. (Davidson was my maiden name before I married in 1955.)

On Saturdays Steve Oyakawa and another apprentice set up shop for giving haircuts. Here Bill Patrick has his hair cut.

Paolo Soleri, peeling potatoes. Paolo now has his own fellowship, called "Arcosanti," in Arizona. He also designs and makes elaborate bells which are sold all over the world.

One day I was given a jeepload of oranges and grapefruit, a 100-pound sack of sugar, and a recipe for making marmalade. I had never made marmalade before. Here are the results in the kitchen.

Another time I was appointed breakfast cook, requiring a 5.00 a.m. start, before the generators for electricity were turned on. I had to stir the pancake batter with one hand while holding a flashlight with the other. In the Fellowship we learned that one could accomplish anything if one plunged into new projects and solved both large and small problems one by one.

A memorial to Mrs. Wright's daughter, Svetlana, who was killed in a car accident. Mr. Wright later used this same design concept when planning the Huntington Hartford Project in 1947. One circular area of this project was used for the theater, another for the dining area, and the third for the swimming pool.

Mr. and Mrs. Wright's rooms, with Mr. Wright's sleeping bag in the foreground. Blocks were added to the facia to cast shadow patterns that mimicked the shadows of rocks on the desert. These lines were dotted rather than straight.

Mr. and Mrs. Wright's study

These stairs led to a deck above the kitchen.

The "guest deck"—a series of small rooms resembling cabins on a ship. The many guests who came to visit Taliesin West stayed here.

Often parties were held on weekends, and we all dressed up for these occasions. In the foreground is Shao Fang, the wife of Sheng Pao, who was a fine artist. Sheng Pao died years ago. Shoa Fang lives in West Virginia, where she continues her work as an artist and teacher.

Mr. and Mrs. Wright, their family, and the apprentices with their spouses and children—having Easter breakfast.

The chorus performing at Easter breakfast.

Mr. and Mrs. Wright

This car was available to be used by anyone who could make it go. John Pel and Michel Marx had managed to get us this far.

This car had formerly been a convertible. Its top had been damaged in an accident, so Mr. Wright took the opportunity to design and construct a new one. He said he had always wanted to design a car, and this gave him the chance to design at least part of one.

Mr. and Mrs. Wright enjoying their new sports car, which was painted to match the trim on the architecture. Mrs. Wright did the driving.

Here Mr. Wright is wearing his favorite jacket. This jacket is still in the Taliesin archives, among all the drawings and other treasures of Taliesin and Taliesin West.